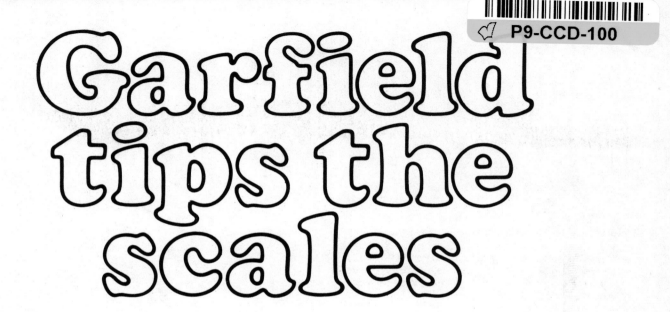

Garfield tips the scales

BY: JIM DAVIS

BALLANTINE BOOKS · NEW YORK

Library of Congress Catalog Card Number: 83-91152
ISBN 0-345-31271-6

Manufactured in the United States of America

First Edition: March 1984

10 9 8 7 6 5 4 3 2 1

GARFIELD'S 10 ALL-TIME FAVORITE BAD CAT JOKES

1 Q: What do you get when you cross a cat with a fish?
A: A carp that always lands on its feet.

2 Q: What does a cat take for a bad memory?
A: Milk of Amnesia.

3 Q: Did you hear about the two cats who were inseparable?
A: They were Siamese twins.

4 Q: Why did the cat climb the drapes?
A: He had good claws to.

5 Q: Did you hear about the cat who was an over-achiever?
A: He had 10 lives.

6 Q: Why do cats eat fur balls?
A: They love a good gag.

7 Q: Did you hear about the cat who made a killing in sports?
A: He was in the tennis racket.

8 I knew a cat who was so rich . . . he had his mice monogrammed.

9 Q: What do you get when you cross a cat with a dog?
A: A badly injured dog.

10 Q: Can cats see in the dark?
A: Yes, but they have trouble holding the flashlight.

CRUNCH
CRUNCH
CRUNCH

JIM DAVIS   8-16

I KNOW YOU'RE HUNGRY, GARFIELD

CRUNCH
CRUNCH

BUT WHAT SAY I BOIL THAT SPAGHETTI FIRST?

IT IS A TAD FIRM

I'LL SEE YOU LATER, GARFIELD. I'M GOING TO THE SUPERMARKET

JIM DAVIS   8-17

LET'S SEE... I HAVE MY SHOPPING LIST, MY KEYS...

DON'T FORGET YOUR SHOPPING BAG

SUPERMARKETS ARE LIKE A GIANT UNITED NATIONS OF FOOD

YOU HAVE COFFEE FROM BRAZIL, CHEESE FROM FRANCE, BEEF FROM AUSTRALIA...

AND LASAGNA FROM HEAVEN

© 1982 United Feature Syndicate, Inc.

ONE FROZEN LASAGNA

TWO FROZEN PIZZAS

© 1982 United Feature Syndicate, Inc.

ONE FROZEN PASTA FREAK

LOOK OUT, WORLD! HERE COMES THE CAPED AVENGER!

JIM DAVIS 8-30

OH, SURE, SUPER-HERO CRIME FIGHTERS MAKE FOR AN OLD, OVERUSED STORY LINE...

BUT HAVE YOU EVER HEARD OF A FAT, WEAK ONE?

© 1982 United Feature Syndicate, Inc.

THE CAPED AVENGER STEPS INTO THE SEAMY UNDERWORLD AND REASSERTS HIS NOBLE CODE

JIM DAVIS 8-31

"I WILL SEEK OUT EVIL WHEREVER IT MAY LURK AND DESTROY IT"

UNLESS, OF COURSE, THERE IS THE SLIGHTEST POSSIBILITY OF HARM TO MY PERSON

© 1982 United Feature Syndicate, Inc.

THE CAPED AVENGER SPOTS SOME EVIL THAT MUST BE SEVERELY DEALT WITH

9-5

JIM DAVIS

WHAM!

BIFF!

BAM!

THE CAPED AVENGER WOULD BE A MORE EFFECTIVE CRIME FIGHTER IF HE DIDN'T HAVE TO USE ONE HAND TO HOLD HIS CAPE UP

© 1982 United Feature Syndicate, Inc.

THIS CAPE IS THE SOURCE OF MY POWER, THE SOURCE OF MY IDENTITY

JIM DAVIS

9-4

THE SOURCE OF MY SECURITY

© 1982 United Feature Syndicate, Inc.

AS LONG AS I'M IMPROVING MYSELF THIS WEEK, I MIGHT AS WELL TRY TO GET ALONG WITH ODIE

JIM DAVIS

COME HERE, ODIE. GIVE ME A BIG HUG

9-8

© 1982 United Feature Syndicate, Inc.

YUK

I SHALL NOW USE SHEER WILLPOWER TO RESIST EATING THAT HAMBURGER

9-9

JIM DAVIS

UNNNGH

WAH!

I'M BEGINNING TO WORRY ABOUT GARFIELD

© 1982 United Feature Syndicate, Inc.

THIS SELF-IMPROVEMENT BIT IS BEGINNING TO BUG ME. I FEEL LIKE A GOODY-TWO-SHOES

JIM DAVIS 9-10

MAYBE MY OLD PERSONALITY WASN'T ALL THAT BAD...

THE GLUTTONY, LAZINESS AND CYNICISM LENT A LITTLE TEXTURE

© 1982 United Feature Syndicate, Inc.

I'M SICK OF THIS SELF-IMPROVEMENT KICK

9-11 JIM DAVIS

I'M FAT, I'M LAZY, AND I'M CYNICAL!

I ADMIRE THAT IN A CAT

© 1982 United Feature Syndicate, Inc.

WHAP!

CHUKING

CATCH, GARFIELD

BONK!

EVER HAVE A DAY WHEN YOUR TIMING WAS ALL OFF?

JIM DAVIS 9-12

© 1982 United Feature Syndicate, Inc.

© 1982 United Feature Syndicate, Inc.

A VERY SHORT BUT NEAT RAIN SHOWER

SPLAT

© 1982 United Feature Syndicate, Inc.

LOOK AT ALL THOSE TINY ANTS GOING TO THE TINY BEACH TO DO SOME SWIMMING

JiM DAViS   9-25

UH-OH. A TINY MINNOW IS CRUISING IN TO EAT THE SWIMMERS

UH-OH. THE MINNOW JUST GOT HARPOONED BY AN ANT WHO BEARS A STRIKING RESEMBLANCE TO ROBERT SHAW

© 1982 United Feature Syndicate, Inc.

-WHAM!
-WHAM!

© 1982 United Feature Syndicate, Inc.

JIM DAVIS 9-26

OH NO! IT'S NOT THERE!

JIM DAVIS 9-27

I'M NOT GETTING OUT OF BED WITHOUT IT!

NOT WITHOUT MY MORNING CUP OF COFFEE

© 1982 United Feature Syndicate, Inc.

GOOD MORNING, JON

JIM DAVIS 9-28

WELL HELLOOOO THERE. COME TO PAPA

THAT'S ME, JON ARBUCKLE, SECOND FIDDLE TO A COFFEE BEAN

© 1982 United Feature Syndicate, Inc.

10-3

© 1982 United Feature Syndicate, Inc.

JIM DAVIS

IMAGINE, THE NERVE OF JON GIVING ME A DUMMY AS A COMPANION. WHAT KIND OF AN INTELLECTUAL DWARF DOES HE THINK I AM?

JIM DAVIS   10-8

PRACTICE OF THE ARISTOTELIAN MEAN WOULD HAVE A SIGNIFICANT POSITIVE EFFECT ON THE WORLD INSTITUTIONAL ENVIRONMENT

© 1982 United Feature Syndicate, Inc.

OH, SHUT UP

YOUR LITTLE FRIEND HERE IS CERTAINLY CUTE, GARFIELD

JIM DAVIS   10-9

STOMP!
STOMP!
STOMP!

LITTLE FRIEND OR NOT, THERE'S SOMETHING TO BE SAID FOR THE DIPLOMATIC REMOVAL OF COMPETITION

© 1982 United Feature Syndicate, Inc.

HERE'S AN INTERESTING ARTICLE ABOUT THE ANCIENT PRACTICE OF CANNIBALISM

LOVELY

CAN YOU IMAGINE WHAT LIFE WAS LIKE THEN?

TRAVELING SALESMEN WERE CALLED "MEALS ON WHEELS"

HAVING THE BOSS OVER FOR DINNER HAD AN ENTIRELY DIFFERENT MEANING

IT SAYS HERE CERTAIN TRIBAL SOCIETIES ALSO ATE CATS

© 1982 United Feature Syndicate, Inc.

I CAN HEAR A DINER COMPLAINING, "OH, WAITER, THERE'S A FLEA COLLAR IN MY SOUP"

THAT'S NOT FUNNY

JIM DAVIS   10-10

MY NOSE WAS WET

WHAT A WARM AND WONDERFUL GESTURE

I LOVE IT WHEN YOU CUDDLE UP TO ME, GARFIELD

© 1982 United Feature Syndicate, Inc.

JIM DAVIS 10-16

© 1982 United Feature Syndicate, Inc.

I LOVE ME, TOO

JIM DAVIS 10-15

I COULD TELL YOU I LOVE YOU

I UNDERSTAND HOW YOU FEEL

I WISH YOU UNDERSTOOD MY EVERY WORD, GARFIELD

I WONDER WHAT KIND OF HAT THIS IS?

WHAT TIME'S THAT THERE BUS LEAVING FOR TOPEKA?

SEE YUH, MOM. BILLY BOB AND ME ARE GONNA PLAY IN TRAFFIC

GEE, I'D LOVE TO GO TO THE COTILLION BUT I GOTTA STAY HOME AND WATCH ARM-WRESTLING ON TV

10-24

JIM DAVIS

THAT'S IT. THIS MUST BE ONE OF THOSE STUPID HATS

STOP HANGING AROUND ME, KID. JUST REMEMBER, YOU'RE A TENDER YOUNG CHICKEN AND I'M A VERY HUNGRY CAT

JIM DAVIS 11-5

I GUESS I GAVE THAT LITTLE GIBLET THE WHAT FOR

EYOW!

© 1982 United Feature Syndicate, Inc.

FOR THE LAST TIME, KID. I'M NOT YOUR DADDY. YOU'RE A CHICKEN AND I'M A CAT

JIM DAVIS 11-6

NOW GO BACK TO YOUR MOTHER

GOODBYE, DADDY

© 1982 United Feature Syndicate, Inc.

GARFIELD'S LAW: CATS INSTINCTIVELY KNOW THE PRECISE MOMENT THEIR OWNERS WILL AWAKE...

© 1982 United Feature Syndicate, Inc.

11-10

THEN THEY AWAKEN THEM TEN MINUTES SOONER

GARFIELD'S LAW: CATS ARE NATURALLY ATTRACTED TO ONLY ONE TYPE OF HUMAN BEING...

11-11

© 1982 United Feature Syndicate, Inc.

THE TYPE WHO IS ALLERGIC TO CATS

WAHCHOO!

GARFIELD'S LAW: CATS CAN'T HEAR COMMANDS...

GARFIELD! GET OFF THE BED!

JIM DAVIS 11-12

CATS CAN'T UNDERSTAND CAJOLING...

SEE? EVEN TOMMY THE CLOWN LIKES THIS NEW CAT FOOD

GARFIEL

© 1982 United Feature Syndicate, Inc.

BUT THEY DO SENSE WHEN YOU WANT TO TAKE THEM TO THE VET

LET'S GO FOR A RIDE, GARFIELD

GARFIELD'S LAW: CATS SHED IN DIRECT PROPORTION TO THEIR CONTRAST WITH A PERSON'S SUIT

JIM DAVIS 11-15

© 1982 United Feature Syndicate, Inc.

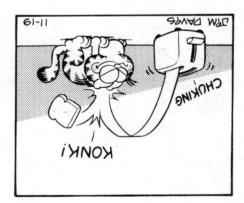

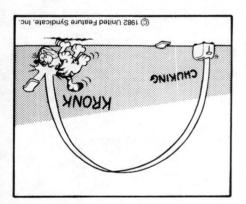

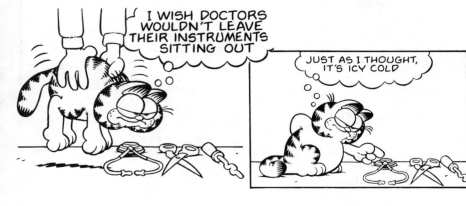

I WISH DOCTORS WOULDN'T LEAVE THEIR INSTRUMENTS SITTING OUT

JUST AS I THOUGHT, IT'S ICY COLD

I WONDER WHAT SHE INTENDS TO SNIP OFF WITH THIS?

© 1982 United Feature Syndicate, Inc.

I DON'T EVEN WANT TO KNOW WHERE THIS GOES

HELLO, GARFIELD

ARRRGH!

JIM DAVIS

HE'S FAINTED DEAD AWAY

HE'S DADDY'S LITTLE TROOPER

11-21

OH, GEE, I CAN'T GET INTO MY BED WITH THESE MUDDY FEET

Z

11-22

JIM DAVIS

© 1982 United Feature Syndicate, Inc.

I LOVE TO SLEEP. I SLEEP TO RESTORE MY ENERGY

JIM DAVIS

I SLEEP TO REFRESH MY WITS

11-23

I SLEEP TO ESCAPE

© 1982 United Feature Syndicate, Inc.

Z

GARFIELD! WHAT HAPPENED?

I HAD A NAP ATTACK AT FULL THROTTLE

JIM DAVIS   11-24

© 1982 United Feature Syndicate, Inc.

IF I WERE TO COME BACK TO THIS EARTH, I'D LIKE TO COME BACK AS A PILLOW

I COULD LIE IN BED ALL DAY

JIM DAVIS

AND PEOPLE WOULD PUT THEIR HEADS IN MY LAP AND GO TO SLEEP

© 1982 United Feature Syndicate, Inc.   11-25

SNAP! —
SQUEAK!
WHAT'S THAT?

JIM DAVIS   11-29

OH, NO! SINCE I'M NOT A MOUSER, JON SET A MOUSETRAP. NOW IT'S KILLED A MOUSE!

© 1982 United Feature Syndicate, Inc.

IF YOU DID YOUR JOB, I WOULDN'T BE IN THIS FIX

I'M SORRY YOU GOT CAUGHT IN THAT MOUSETRAP, MOUSE

OH, THAT'S OKAY. I HAVE A WIFE AND EIGHT KIDS

JIM DAVIS   11-30

WHAT DOES THAT HAVE TO DO WITH ANYTHING?

THIS IS THE FIRST PEACE AND QUIET I'VE HAD IN YEARS

© 1982 United Feature Syndicate, Inc.

© 1982 United Feature Syndicate, Inc.

12-3

© 1982 United Feature Syndicate, Inc.

12-4

DON'T KNOCK THOSE FLOWERS OFF THE WINDOWSILL, GARFIELD

I PUT THEM THERE TO GIVE THEM SOME SUN

AND SOME FRESH AIR

12-6

© 1982 United Feature Syndicate, Inc.

WINDOWS ARE GREAT. THEY OFFER A FRONT ROW SEAT TO LIFE'S PASSING PARADE

JIM DAVIS   12-7

THUD!

© 1982 United Feature Syndicate, Inc.

THEY ARE ALSO GOOD FOR A YUK OR TWO

BOOM
BOOM
BOOM

JIM DAVIS   12-13

BOOM   BOOM   BOOM

IT'S TIME YOU WENT ON ANOTHER DIET, GARFIELD

ON THIS DIET, GARFIELD, YOU MAY DRINK ALL THE COFFEE YOU PLEASE

JIM DAVIS   12-14

GULP
GULP
GULP

THIS IS SOME KIND OF WEIRD DIET

SLOSH

SLOSH

SLOSH

SLOSH

GOOD MORNING, GARFIELD. IS THERE SOMETHING YOU'RE TRYING TO TELL ME?

JIM DAVIS

© 1982 United Feature Syndicate, Inc.

IT'S THE CHRISTMAS SEASON, YOU SAY

12-20

GIMME, GIMME, GIMME, GIMME, GIMME, GIMME, GIMME, GIMME

JIM DAVIS   12-21

GIMME! GIMME! GIMME! GIMME! GIMME! GIMME!

I'M GETTING INTO THE CHRISTMAS SPIRIT

© 1982 United Feature Syndicate, Inc.

NIBBLE
NIBBLE
NIBBLE

12-29   JIM DAVIS

IT'S NOT GOOD TO CHEW YOUR NAILS, GARFIELD

OH, THAT'S OKAY

I'M CHEWING ON ODIE'S

© 1982 United Feature Syndicate, Inc.

Z

JIM DAVIS   12-30

I'M BORED. I NEED TO ADD SOME SPARKLE TO MY LIFE

Z

© 1982 United Feature Syndicate, Inc.

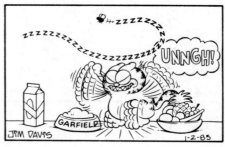

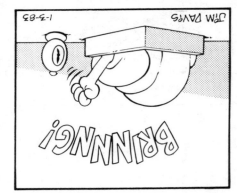

© 1983 United Feature Syndicate, Inc.

© 1983 United Feature Syndicate, Inc.

HEY, ODIE, WOULD YOU LIKE TO PLAY BALL?

SQUEAK

© 1963 United Feature Syndicate, Inc.

TIE
TIE

HEY, GARFIELD, WHERE'S ODIE?

HE'S TIED UP AT THE MOMENT

DRIBBLE
DRIBBLE
DRIBBLE

JIM DAVIS   1-9

SLAM

1-10 JIM DAVIS

HEY, GARFIELD. I'M HOME

YOU'RE CERTAINLY EXCITED TO SEE ME

BELIEVE ME, INSIDE I'M HOPPING UP AND DOWN AND SHOUTING WITH GLEE

© 1983 United Feature Syndicate, Inc.

SO I SAY TO THIS CLERK, "LOOK, IF THE WHOLE BUNCH OF BANANAS IS 54 CENTS, WHY CAN'T I HAVE ONE FOR 6 CENTS?"

1-11 JIM DAVIS

© 1983 United Feature Syndicate, Inc.

DON'T YOU WANT TO HEAR HOW THE STORY CAME OUT?

TELL IT TO YOUR PLANTS

GARFIELD, YOU SEEM TO BE PREOCCUPIED THIS WEEK

HUH?

© 1983 United Feature Syndicate, Inc.

GARFIELD HASN'T BEEN LISTENING TO ME LATELY. WATCH THIS

HEY, GARFIELD, WHAT SAY WE GO TO THE VET AND GET YOU DECLAWED?

THAT WOULD BE FINE

CASE CLOSED

© 1983 United Feature Syndicate, Inc.

I HATE IT WHEN GARFIELD IGNORES ME

1-14 JIM DAVIS

DARN IT! PAY SOME ATTENTION TO ME!

Z

I THINK I'M GOING TO CRY

© 1983 United Feature Syndicate, Inc.

JON, I KNOW I'VE BEEN IGNORING YOU LATELY, BUT I WANT TO SAY IT'S NOT BECAUSE I DON'T CARE FOR YOU

1-15

IT'S LIKE MY EARS HEAR YOU, BUT MY BRAIN KEEPS STRAYING OFF COURSE. I'VE JUST BEEN PREOCCUPIED

JIM DAVIS © 1983 United Feature Syndicate, Inc.

ENOUGH SAID. LET'S GET ON WITH IT

HUH?

I LOVE IT WHEN THEY ENTERTAIN ME

IT APPEARS JON HAS PREPARED HIMSELF A VERY NICE MEAL, BUT SOMETHING IS MISSING. WHAT COULD IT BE?

WHY, OF COURSE...

THE CAT HAIR!

WHIRRR!

NIGHTIE-NIGHT, JON

I HATE YOU

1-26

SURPRISE, GARFIELD! I BOUGHT YOU ANOTHER RUBBER MOUSE

YIPPEE SKIP

BY THE WAY, WHAT HAPPENED TO YOUR LAST ONE?

IT WAS TRAGIC

HE WAS CAUGHT AND EATEN BY A RUBBER CAT

1-27

SURPRISE, GARFIELD! I THREW YOUR OLD BED IN THE TRASH AND GOT YOU THIS NEW ONE. WHAT DO YOU THINK?

JIM DAVIS

1-28

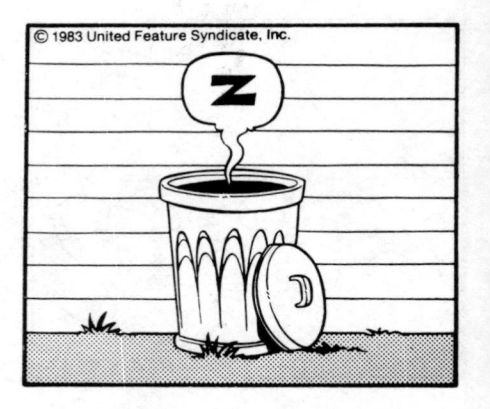

Z

DOGS HAVE THE WORLD'S STUPIDEST TOYS. JUST LOOK AT THIS RUBBER BONE

JIM DAVIS

SIMPLE MINDS, SIMPLE PLEASURES

IT CERTAINLY DOESN'T HOLD THE SCINTILLATING INTELLECTUAL CHALLENGE OF MY FUZZY SCRATCHING POST WITH THE SPRINGY RUBBER MOUSIE

1-29

© 1983 United Feature Syndicate, Inc.

JIM DAVIS 1-30

ROWR!

ARRRGH!

THAT WASN'T FUNNY, GARFIELD!

FUNNY IS IN THE EYE OF THE BEHOLDER

2-2 JIM DAVIS

I SEWED POOKY'S ARM BACK ON AS GOOD AS NEW, GARFIELD

YES, BUT WILL HE EVER PLAY THE PIANO AGAIN?

ME THINKS THE CAT DOTH EXPECT TOO MUCH

© 1983 United Feature Syndicate, Inc.

YOU DID A PRETTY GOOD JOB OF SEWING POOKY'S ARM ON

2-3 JIM DAVIS

I USED SMALL STITCHES SO AS NOT TO LEAVE A SCAR

I THINK HE'S PICKING ON ME

© 1983 United Feature Syndicate, Inc.

I CAN STARE
ANYTHING
DOWN

UH, GARFIELD,
FISH CAN'T
BLINK

NOW HE TELLS ME...
NOW THAT MY EYEBALLS
ARE ALL DRIED OUT

JIM DAVIS   2-6

© 1983 United Feature Syndicate, Inc

ARE YOU SURE YOU WANT TO WATCH THIS, GARFIELD?

JIM DAVIS

IT'S A DEPRESSING MOVIE ABOUT A MAN-EATING LION THAT TERRORIZES A NATIVE VILLAGE

2-14

YOU ROOT FOR YOUR SIDE, I'LL ROOT FOR MINE

LION

© 1983 United Feature Syndicate, Inc.

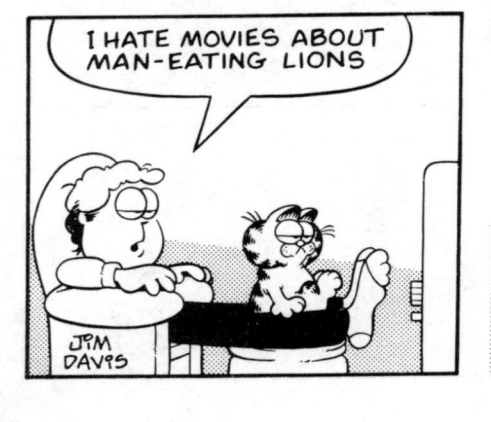

I HATE MOVIES ABOUT MAN-EATING LIONS

JIM DAVIS

HOW CAN AN ANIMAL POSSIBLY PREY ON AN INNOCENT VICTIM?

2-15

EXPLAIN THAT TO THE CHICKEN YOU HAD FOR DINNER

© 1983 United Feature Syndicate, Inc.

OH, NO! THE LION RAN DOWN ANOTHER VILLAGER!

THE ORIGINAL FAST-FOOD FRANCHISE

NOW WHAT DISGUSTING THING IS THE LION DOING?

2-16

HE'S SPITTING THE SPEAR OUT

© 1983 United Feature Syndicate, Inc.

TELL ME WHEN THE LION IS FINISHED EATING THE VILLAGER, OKAY, GARFIELD?

YOU CAN LOOK NOW

EEEEEK!

2-17

HE WASN'T DONE YET!

OH, I THOUGHT YOU MEANT THE MAIN PARTS

© 1983 United Feature Syndicate, Inc.

GOOD! THEY SHOT THE LION!

WHAT DO YOU THINK OF THOSE APPLES, GARFIELD?

BIG DEAL

2-18

AT THE GUN IT WAS VILLAGERS: 1, LION: 42

© 1983 United Feature Syndicate, Inc.

WELL, WHAT DID YOU THINK OF THE MAN-EATING LION MOVIE?

2-19

YOU KNOW I HATE THAT, GARFIELD

© 1983 United Feature Syndicate, Inc.

© 1983 United Feature Syndicate, Inc.

JIM DAVIS   2-20

THIS IS CALLED A BIRD FEEDER, GARFIELD

JIM DAVIS 2-25

AND THIS IS CALLED PUTTING BIRDSEED INTO THE BIRD FEEDER

HE CAN CALL IT WHAT HE LIKES. I CALL IT BAITING THE TRAP

WOW! LOOK AT ALL THIS GOOD FOOD AND NEAT CLOTHING!

2-26

THIS IS GREAT STUFF

STAY OUT OF THE TRASH, GARFIELD

HOW DID YOU KNOW?

JIM DAVIS

JIM DAVIS 2·27

© 1983 United Feature Syndicate, Inc.

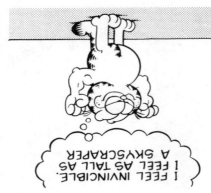

3-6

UH-OH, THERE'S A PACKAGE FOR ME

JIM DAVIS   3-7

I DON'T THINK I'M GOING TO LIKE IT

BEWARE OF GIFTS BEARING AIR HOLES

© 1983 United Feature Syndicate, Inc.

GEE, I HOPE THIS PACKAGE DOESN'T HAVE A BOMB OR A MONSTER IN IT

JIM DAVIS   3-8

GASP! IT'S EVEN WORSE THAN MY MOST HIDEOUS FEARS!

IT'S ANOTHER SWEATER FOR ME FROM JON'S MOTHER

© 1983 United Feature Syndicate, Inc.

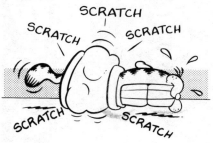

JON SURE LOOKS DUMB WITH HIS FAKE MUSTACHE

VERY FEW PEOPLE CAN WEAR A MUSTACHE

JIM DAVIS   3-16

© 1983 United Feature Syndicate, Inc.

LIKE EVIL ROY GATO, FOR INSTANCE

NYAH, NYAH, NYAAAH, EVIL ROY GATO DOES HIS DAILY DIRTY DEED

JIM DAVIS   3-17

PUSH

THE MUSTACHE MADE ME DO IT

OH, THERE YOU ARE, GARFIELD

JIM DAVIS 3-18

LET ME GUESS...YOU STOLE MY FAKE MUSTACHE AND ATE MY SPAGHETTI, RIGHT?

HOW'D YOU GUESS?

© 1983 United Feature Syndicate, Inc.

GIVE ME A KISS, SWEETHEART

JIM DAVIS 3-19

KISS

HOW DO YOU TELL A LADY HER MUSTACHE NEEDS MORE WAX?

© 1983 United Feature Syndicate, Inc.

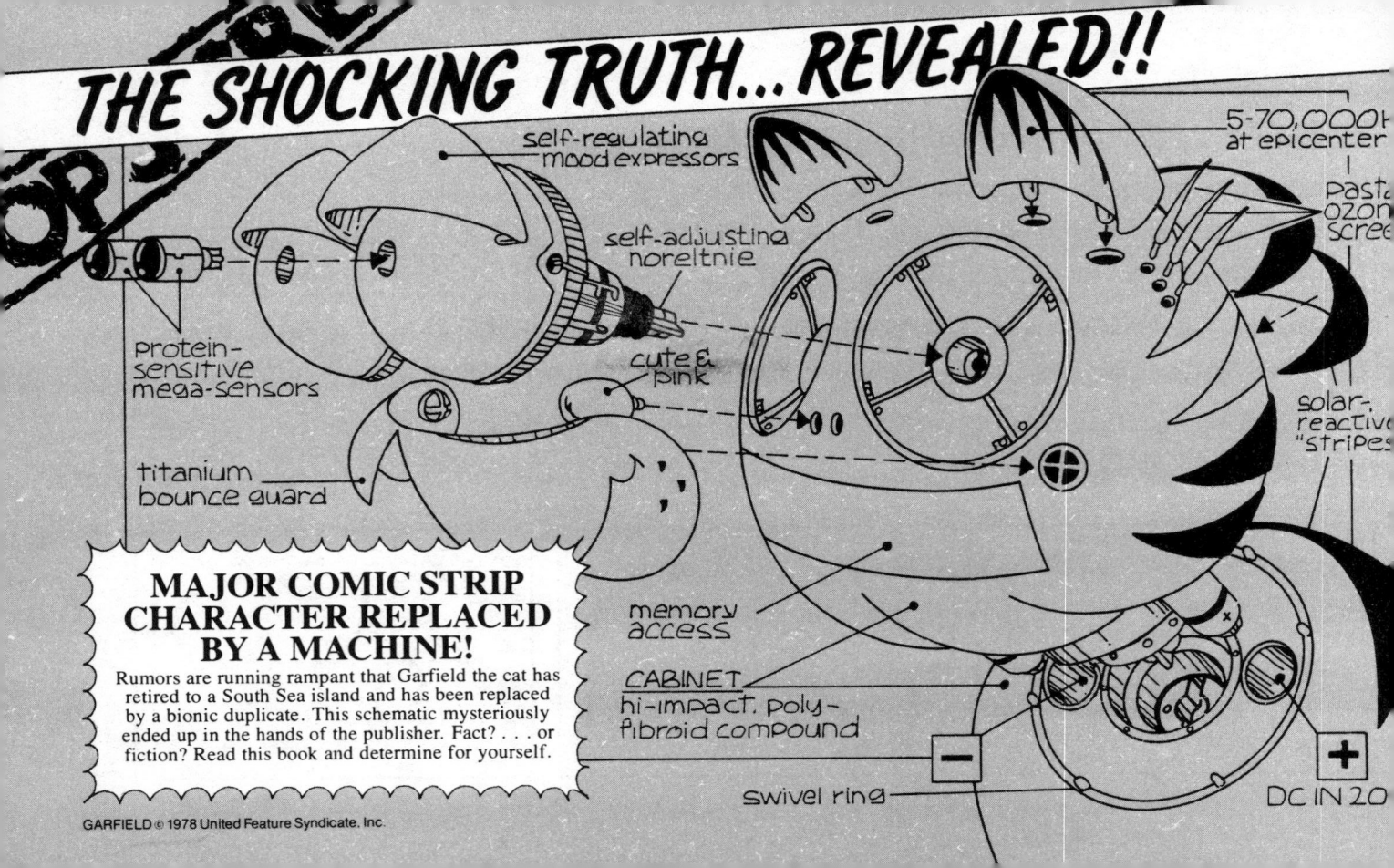

THE SHOCKING TRUTH... REVEALED!!

self-regulating mood expressors

self-adjusting noreltnie

5-70,000 at epicenter

pasta ozone screen

protein-sensitive mega-sensors

cute & pink

titanium bounce guard

solar-reactive "stripes"

MAJOR COMIC STRIP CHARACTER REPLACED BY A MACHINE!

Rumors are running rampant that Garfield the cat has retired to a South Sea island and has been replaced by a bionic duplicate. This schematic mysteriously ended up in the hands of the publisher. Fact? . . . or fiction? Read this book and determine for yourself.

memory access

CABINET hi-impact, poly-fibroid compound

swivel ring

DC IN 20